Endorsements are coming

"I thoroughly enjoyed reading *The Being & Becoming Book*. The writings are filled with inspiration and deserve more than just one reading. I would recommend that this book be read a piece at a time. I have found in doing this, my own being and becoming was assisted by these wonderful expressions of light. Thank you!"

~ Rev. Michael J. Brooks
Unity of The White Mountains, AZ

"Cynthia Clayton is in service to the radical spiritual awakening that is accelerating amongst us today. Her book, *The Being & Becoming Book*, seems to me a collection of pointers to this unflawed, unrestricted essence, which is our truest nature... the awakening to which is freedom from domination by the little, needy, fictitious self that had imprisoned so many of us. Read it and see what happens."

~ Rev. Mark Pope, Unity Church of Sedona, AZ;
Founder of The Awakening Heart Center,
Author of For the Aspiring Mystic

"Inspirational and insightful. Cindy offers a thought provoking poetic ride through her personal reflections and experiences. A very enjoyable journey."

~ Rev. Robert Spinden, The Center of Religious Science, Delta, CO
Author of Dancing With The Divine: Unleashing Your Inner Magnificence

"When you read this book, be prepared for a spiritual pilgrimage into yourself through the words of the author. Cynthia Clayton is without a doubt a genius in her interpretation of life and the pursuit of true happiness."

~ Rev. Beverly Parks, Ph.D. in Pastoral Counseling Psychology;
M.S. in Counseling; Master's in Metaphysical Science

The Being & Becoming Book

Unfold
Yourself
Gently

CYNTHIA CLAYTON

Cedar Hill Publishing

The Being & Becoming Book – Unfold Yourself … Gently

Editing and formatting by Rebecca Hayes

Cover design by Rebecca Hayes

Published in the United States by
Cedar Hill Publishing
Snowflake, AZ 85937
www.cedarhillpublishing.com

ISBN-13: 978-0-9816919-9-2

Library of Congress Control Number 2008931021

For ordering information, visit:

www.experiencebeing.com

Friends:

Why are millions of people buying books like The Secret, The Power of Now, A New Earth, *and anything by Wayne Dyer or Deepak Chopra? Because humanity is experiencing an explosive spiritual awakening.*

The Being & Becoming Book *is a journal of my ascension process into a higher level of consciousness. It is full of "Ah-ha" moments, pointers and signposts to open your mind, open your heart and open your soul.*

Merely a portal for these inspirations, I was usually awakened at sunrise, feeling a strong Presence and a connection with All That Is. I know this book was divinely inspired, because I don't do early mornings, and barely got up at dawn to give birth to my children!

These inspirations are powerful beyond words, triggers that resonate in your heart and nestle in that stillness within. You will cry upon realization of your sacredness, become One with the Essence of Life, and be touched by the Grace of the Divine.

This book is not another self-help book, which appeals to the mind. The Being & Becoming Book *is a collection of short reflections that appeal to a deeper level of the spirit, and for this reason, the reader may more quickly awaken.*

Blessings!

Cindy Clayton

Introduction

As you try on these reflections, the fit will be comfortable, because deep down you've worn them before. A part of us feels we have always been, and will always be. A deep part of us feels connected to All That Is, like a wave in the vast ocean of *Being*.

I simply want you to feel good about life, right where you're at, what you're doing, and who you are. I want you to know in the fiber of your bones that *you* are special, just by being alive, and that there is an inherent sanctity to reality.

There are no answers for you here. Would it bother you if there never were any answers to anything? If you knew that, maybe you would cease asking questions, and begin enjoying more peaceful and mindful living. But what I hope finds you in these reflections is yourself. Beyond your little me, your ego, is a greater Self trying to enter your consciousness right now. Find that becoming thing within, fearless and desire-less, and get out of its way. Your transformation is inevitable.

Rather than try fruitlessly to define Life, I'm trying to appreciate It, just the way It is, and just the way I am. I'm trying to show It the respect It deserves. Sounds like I'm in love, don't you think? The All-ness of Life has always been there, waiting for me to catch up.

My motivation for writing this book is to get your feet unstuck from the mud. And my feet. That's all! Start anywhere you like in this book. Like life, this book has no beginning. There may be a BANG here or a birth there, but Life has been going on and on... well... forever. Like life, my book throws bits and pieces at you. Don't try to sort them! Just enjoy the ride. Trust Life to sort Itself out. It knows what It's doing. Trust yourself.

We find ourselves in a visible world of opposites that, like a benevolent magician, always has paradoxes up its sleeves. On the one hand, there are no true beginnings. Any beginning was Itself begotten. But on the other hand, EVERYTHING IS A BEGINNING. Every little thing. Life is always new, becoming, transforming, maneuvering with a propensity to exist, a flair to flourish, to nourish. This nurturing, this creation, is a field of Love, guidance, caring, betterment and encouragement to succeed at being the best life.

So, life is both without beginning and always beginning. Such is the nature of the Manifesting Power. Such is the nature of Eternity. Such is your inherent spiritual nature.

Enter that *Becoming* place...

To warm you up, I begin with a few reflections I wrote while living on a houseboat. Dwelling in silence and beauty, my spirit began unfolding.

After all these years, I remain in awe of the Mystery, and realize I don't need to know it all... I know enough. Life is good, and I appreciate the special journey it allows.

The Summons

Bring to me the poor and weary,
those too tired to sleep or think,
and all the blessed hearts of poets
come here to me to drink.

I shed the light on former problems,
and deepest hopes rekindle new,
I spread the bliss of just pure being,
my soothing magic cradles you.

Look no further, you've got it,
open your heart and see
you're a golden spawn of majestic Creation,
take joy in your heredity!

Prayer for New Awareness

May the magnificent power of the Spirit
ascend from the depths of our hearts.
Let it build a raging fire of love for mankind,
reverence for nature,
vision past the boundaries of civilization,
and eject us into greater consciousness.

To the Creator at Daybreak

Oh, Lighter of Prisms, Beginner of the Diamond,
as colors unfold, in spite of it all, it sure is nice.
Darkness into form, the glitter and magic of dawn.
From where? The center. The center - of me.

The dreams unfold, the dreams and the dreams.
The river always runs, though the snow becomes a hardened crystal.
Take me slow, I want to see it all, I want to know where I'm going
and with whom.
Doesn't the Prince come in the end?

Lighter of Prisms, Beginner of the Diamond, Burner of Bridges,
Chef of the Pot –
this thirst be quenched, I'd rather drop.

Interlude on the Riverbank

Oh, river, may you know the trees;
Oh, river, but may you not linger.
You are leaving and returning to your source.
Does man know his Source?

Why does he constantly search for what's behind form?
The veil will drop.
The mountain will crumble.
And then we shall see
our source is One.

Crossing Over

The desert invades your soul.
It comes into you and takes you over,
offering a loneliness that is welcome
like the sweet death that comes after a long, long sickness.
I have been sick with society for too long.
I have finally crossed over.

The mountains shout at you about their beauty,
but the desert whispers to you,
entices you,
and then, when you come very close,
she snares you.
You sink into her like quicksand and are lost forever, loving her.

As I teetered on a craggy perch
above the blue-green inner sanctum of the river,
gazing across the endless fertile wilderness,
it seemed each breath I took,
when I exhaled, my spirit grew.
It grew immense, until it filled the whole desert.
I was the whole desert,
walking upon it with my soul;
I was One.

This is what the desert does to you
once you dwell with her and learn to love her:
she opens your soul, rips it wide open,
and you are bare with nowhere to go and hide from yourself
in the vast uninterrupted space.

I saw society clearly,
and understood how I'd been brainwashed by the system of things.
You may not want to see yourself as transparently,
but you will.
And you will end up hugging yourself for all your efforts,
and laughing at your seriousness.

Follow the Butterfly

I ache for you young ones
who now see the pitfalls of civilization,
but will soon become part of its slavery.
Golden glitter will dazzle your eyes,
you will lose sight of the butterfly of freedom dancing in the distance,
you will build towers that nature will someday crumble and
accumulate titles that don't make the slightest impression on eternity.
Then, your bones will grow old and begin dissolving
to become the dust of the earth.

The butterflies will turn to dust also,
but they have been free all that time.
They have danced in the wind and sung nature's hymn,
while you boarded yourself up inside a house-box
to keep the wind from mussing your hair
or the rain from chilling you.

Yet as you lay dying, you will cry:
"Let me feel the wind on my face!
Drag me from these silken covers and help me touch the sacred earth...
the pelting rain...
the scorching sun...
to die gazing at the stars, and not these four walls!"

You will weep that you didn't see enough,
didn't love enough,
didn't share enough of your inner self with others,
maybe that you never found the inner self in your busy surface life.

The racks of clothes in your closet,
money and papers of accomplishment in your safe,
mean nothing now.
As your eyes dim, they long to see a grand old tree
just one more time.

Finally,
your spirit will soar
with the freedom you never gave it
in your living days.

Seeking mystery, the mystical, or magic, people crave greater consciousness. Yet despite sincerest efforts and constant reaching, they cannot find that spark in themselves, that glimpse of eternity, that seeks them also. If they would only stop seeking, and listen. Find the quietest, most beautiful place in nature and be alone. The spark, that elusive quality of perfect bliss for which they yearn, will find them.

"It" is merely you. Unfettered you. Free, unbothered, unthinking you, your highest self, that part of you that is divine...

The Stirrings of Immortality

#1

How much did I win in life and how much did I lose?
When life is all spent, it will not matter.
This theater of animation is more grandiose than a game and a gamble,
a measuring of success at various endeavors,
a judgment, a contract,
a step to some heaven or higher arena.
This life is the immortality
that Spirit seeks to experience.
Immortality is the fact that life goes on!
It is this minute, not some future event.

Why be concerned about immortality *someday,*
when because of it we are living today.
We are creating another story,
learning, feeling, being aware of it all,
of our actor's role
of the play.

#2

That Life-Energy chose and made us,
we give thanks.
For we are immortal today!
We signature life with imprints we leave behind,
our actions sown in fertile layers of time.
What quality and intensity of spark,
your essence your statement your final mark,
will *you* relinquish on passing through?

#3

The eternal, unquenchable quest for vim and sparkle
we call personal immortality is a thirst for life,
an exploring, enjoying and loving of life.
Yet immortality is not ours personally.
It is a borrowing,
an expression,
a jubilation that came our way
and let soul essence carve a while on smidgens
of the Great Spirit.

#4

Life is not the countless efforts we laboriously create
to sustain our cultural illusion of life,
our particular mirage of a civilized world.
Life is simply the answer to Itself,
whose very manifestation is a celebration.

Our deepest selves are in tune with life.
We feel Its simple stirrings
when we don't pretend to be someone
and don't care what we have acquired or done.
This Spark of Life resides behind the happy contentedness
that says:
I AM! I am glad to be here!

The world's aggressions can come at me
and my I AM is calm and happy.
The clutches of the world can never gain my deepest self.
I belong to the Spark,
to the Sacred Flame,
to that thimbleful of spirit substance
which sometimes expands within my reservoirs
bringing love and joy
to life.

#5

It is my Spirit I hold in honor,
my sacred and immortal link
to the magic of movement and consciousness,
my coming to Life.

I feel this inner connection
and it gives my life a glow of sanctity.
This splendor has nothing to do with my position,
my roles, or my nature of societal existence.
It manifests when I am at my happiest,
quietest and truest times.
When I flame inside with the glory of living.

#6

Although the non-material spirit essence produces the material,
it is so fine a process that no filter can catch it.
Yet our bodies and earth have caught and held
the residue of Life,
as it swoops
and leaves behind its creative spirit
in the region of our matter and our souls,
the Sacred Spark.
I am no more than that Spark
and no other than that Spark.
I am nature.
I am God's essence and hope.

I am only one star in a billion,
but may someday shine more than others
with the happiness of my self-discovery
and how simple it was.

Reflections on the Spirit

#1

Oh Spirit, how do I sing of you,
justify or reckon you?
Crawling around in my words,
floundering out of water, how can I say it?
When will they feel it?

Why, when I say *spirit*, do people have thoughts of afterlife?
I care not what happens to me after this life
since I have only an inkling of the hereafter.
One's spirit adds riches to the here-and-now.

#2

From where do they think their deepest love flows?
Not their hearts, which only pump blood
and never looked or felt like a valentine.
From what part of humankind comes the undirected love that swells inside
and spurts onto bystanders?
Or the pure love of one soul reaching for another?
This love is the bounty of the Spirit, bubbling with hopes of uniting us,
Its pieces.

#3

For Chris:

Accuse me not of fleeing from the reality of life
or seeking the mysteries of death
because I say, "Yes, human beings have a spirit."
Like a shadow, I cannot leave It behind.
It treks with you and I through desert hills,
but takes away not even one part of my love for you,
my acceptance of fact,
or my reverence for this paradise planet.
It only hopes to add to all of this.
Desiring not to chariot me away to a fantasyland or daydream world,
It wants my awareness of truth even more than you do.
It masks not my eyes with veils, but clears them.
My spirit tags along quietly, seeking no special attention,
coming in part because It longs to be one with your spirit,
my realist, my love.

#4

Spirit longs only to exist,
to be awakened and treated justly,
to manifest when possible in the splendor of nature
or the preciousness of a beautiful soul,
to be handled reverently, enshrined delicately,
enclosed within the very best you.

But, if your spirit is left unheralded for years in a dirty jail,
It leaves only an answering service within you,
taking most of Its essence to other sources of hope,
as you join the legions of the walking dead.

However, there is always the possibility that you remember the Spirit.
It will return if you have cleaned your house for It
and lit the lamp.
Like a growing family,
there is always love for one more in Its infinite nature.

#5

Spirit is a traveler, of which I am only one particle.
Its energy will leave me and vibrate into new life
when my form grows old and disintegrates.
And part of me, (that is not *me* at all), will go on;
it is the Spirit going on, taking some of our best memories.

Life-Spirit is sharing Itself eternally.
I am a part, and a welcome part!
Because I accept Its life with joy
and give It a home.

#6

Seek not to spy on Spirit's holiest rituals
for this is intimidating.
Let It come and go freely,
roam through your vast and open spaces,
breathing at last.
Happy to be held in the center of you,
with your delicate caress of a master for his tiny pet,
whom you may never talk to
but may commune with in your deepest self.

#7

People hurt because the Spirit goes unacknowledged.
We work hard for outer gains, but with inner depth we want
no ripples. The growing pains of spirit, the decision-making
and self-evaluation, are uncomfortable.
It is easier to remain ignorant of our spiritual nature.
For once accepted, the spirit becomes king of our inner
throne. Out of respect, we are demanding of ourselves to
please Him. Judging our acts and thoughts is climbing a
narrow, steep trail. We fall several times into a feeling of
failure, but it is we who push ourselves too hard. Spirit
demands nothing. It forgives us and is anxious to pick us up
and keep us going. We can surely forgive ourselves when
spirit-essence cries: "Begin anew! And again!"

We are children learning,
weighing and balancing until we know what will bring our
spirits great happiness.
Then we can sit at the right hand of the throne,
as sons or daughters, as One.

2007 Journal of Ascension

Beginning February 2007, I began to keep a journal. The following reflections are one year's inspired thoughts about the nameless, eternal All That Is. I use the "G" word often. Just easier. Some thoughts came to me in the middle of the night, most at dawn. I knew all year my consciousness was at a higher level than in my past life, that something was happening. I feel a difference, like I'm living a little in a higher dimension, a more rapid rate of vibration, increased warmth in my heart, more peace, more love, more joy. You may be having similar symptoms, and not realize you are ascending in your evolution. I believe there is accelerated consciousness going on right now, covering the planet and including the living planet. I believe if we look past the illusion of an impending downfall to the light beyond, choose peace over fear no matter what happens, we can bring into existence a new earth. But first, to change ourselves. I hope these pointers help you in the navigation to your spirit. Good traveling!

February 2007

Some mountains you climb will be joyful adventures, leading to majestic overlooks.

Other mountains will cause pain and bruising, as you continuously slip on the shale.

Accept the whole journey - the rainbow is always there when needed.

You know it's been a beautiful day when you watch the sunrise and sunset and feel madly in love all day, but not with anyone in particular. I am drawn to love, and it is drawn to me.

I went to bed consumed by peace, carried not one worry to my pillow, then woke in the silent wee hours. I gazed at a crescent moon outside my window, said "Thank you," and returned to the profound sleep of a newborn. At dawn, I basked in radiant sunrise colors coming for me through the window. I was an inherent part of nature's rhythm of life.

I awoke one night, feeling an immortal love in my heart, and wrote:
    This temple is for God. It's not as clean or well lit as it should be, but it bursts with joy at the guest within.

I'm struck by the last line of a movie, the words of a dying man:

I don't know if life is greater than death,
but I know that love is greater than both.

How true, I thought.

The unnamable becomes everything with a name.
"Beyond" concept evolves into *all* concepts.
And yet, the Fountainhead retains all potency, loses nothing,
is the eternal fountain of creative waters.

Most people don't enjoy the surprise of their self-unfolding, because they don't allow their selves to exist. They are who they think they should be, striving to be some image they have selected, or they become who they are expected to be by others. They don't just open up and see what's there. Touch-feel-experience all the moods of Being, and feel harmony at the variety and depth they find. The self is beyond definition, and limitless. It resides in eternity.

So why would you want to be anything at all? Just take the tour.

Love In The Sky

One evening, there was a brilliant sunset. Even Crayola makers couldn't name those colors. I saw a big red heart directly in the center of it. I don't know if any other sunset watchers caught the inference, but the word "LOVE" was attached below the heart. It was a Love's gas station. But to top it off, beneath it was a road sign with a peculiar arrow pointed up to the sky!

I felt love vibrating in the air, and in me, as I gazed at that sign amidst saturated swirling colors. And I felt the warmth of being loved by the Divine. I have loved the Creator for years, but never felt it returned to me in such a manner. My pores absorbed It, my essence was consumed by It, It reached my biology deep within, and I felt an immense spiritual connection to the universe. My heart was opening.

Yes, believe it or not, I was inspired by a gas station sign.

Our purpose on earth is to learn to love. The source of our being is grounded in an energy field of love. In the growing and flowing of love, we have more need to love than to be loved. To let it come out from within our hearts, to rewire our connection to the Divine. True love is unconditional and universal, wants nothing, expects nothing, and is for the universe. It spurts out onto strangers, because there are no strangers when we are all joined at the hip in the rhythm of this Oneness dance.

That this environment of love surrounds us is no doubt. But our connectors are rusty, and we need to take steps in the direction of our inner light. Many spiritual teachers have come and told us how to live by love.

We know how to be; we have known it for years. But we need to progres.
from talking the talk to walking the walk. We need to *be* love, become the
change we wish to see in the world, lovers of earth and humanity, lovers of
our Source, and of ourselves.

We are compelled to love everyone, not because we are told to by
some religion, but because we personally, deeply, must do it. Others are us!
All organisms in the same environment are One entity, all related, relatives
of some sort or another. SO, we have to love the whole shebang! See?

Now. Go watch for the signposts along *your* heart's awakening.

When the Summons comes,
you will know.
"But what if I miss It?"
"I will call again," whispers your heart.

I love the love of God in you. I love the love of God in me.

We were all focused on the Divine.
It felt as if we were one mind.
And as our level of love rose,
we then became one heart.
Though our hearts burned,
our minds felt emptied of thoughts. Peaceful.

Consciousness is not something in the void. It is the Void Itself.

What I Am Not

I know I am not my body. I appreciate, even love it, it gives me pleasure, and experiences a multitude of fun and adventures; it's my encapsulated earthly playsuit. But it is not "I".

"I" is a little more than my body.

My scientific mind, full of information, impulses, plans and constant activity (they say we have a minimum of 20,000 thoughts a day - no wonder we're tired!) is not "I". Very useful and entertaining, though.

What's gathered on my property - the house, cars, furniture, clothes, money, and jewelry - are not "I". They don't travel with my spirit. Too heavy!

My reputation - what others think of me - is not "I". Who knows what they think "I" really am. I don't even know, how could what they assume to know be important or true?

My job is not "I". Money may make the world go around, but love is a better alignment of resources, and more connected to Source.

So what "I Am" seems to be more and more what I am not. More a peeling away of the petals of the rose. And what is left? That silent space between the notes of music, from which all sounds are born. A place of no words, no things, where life continues burning, creating, loving and playing, flourishing, expanding, providing for All. That's where I Am is born, and where "I" return.

March 2007

I feel sorry for my ego, my little self. It has such an important task of maneuvering me through my lessons in life. When the time comes, it will be like saying goodbye to my best friend. If I stop holding onto anger and disappointment, I will have measurably cut back its workload. I wonder how it truly feels about that?

The Night My Ego Cracked Open

I humbly kneeled and cried, I held my heart, I don't know how long I was on the floor. Feelings I had blamed on others, then blamed on myself, I accepted and released. That night in the wee hours, I had a shift in consciousness. My ego cracked open. Finally, I felt a weight lifting, then I began walking on a cloud, living from a totally different viewpoint. What had happened to me?

At lunch with some friends that day, I had decided to symbolically leave any unpleasant feelings in the breadbasket when I left, like an offering. There was a twinge of anger, a tad of disappointment, and a slight feeling of being used.

I see now, that when I woke that night, it was a reckoning with my ego. Who was I really angry at? If I were going to be angry at everyone who acted less than perfect, I'd be mad all day long! Where do I draw the line?? I was essentially angry at myself (my little self, of course), for reacting to others. For letting my buttons be pushed. For even having buttons. I was angry at being angry! Now that seemed ridiculous.

But. If I am Being, being me, how can I be mad at myself unfolding? And, if I am Being in my core, there is really no personal *me* to get angry at! It's just my role in the play. There is no *me* there, and to be angry at thin air seems silly.

When I examined my feeling of being used, I found I was not so much letting others use me, as I was using myself incorrectly. *I* am responsible for my use, allowing how I am rationed out. I can say "yes" or "no". So I was also angry at myself for being wishy-washy.

Finally, the disappointment. Ultimately, it too was with myself. For only I allow myself to go on and on in stagnant conditions.

But my choices and situations are my sacred journey! If I am Being, being me, I am right where I am supposed to be, in my right and perfect place, now. I can't be disappointed in my being-ness! It is wrong, almost cruel, and seemingly irreverent. It would not be loving my Self, a borrowed manifestation of no less or other than the Great Spirit.

I refuse to be disappointed in my life as it blossoms forth. I can't be angry or disappointed in the Divine flow in my life. My ego must be curtailed. It was clear to me that night, that the emotionality, drama, and positionality within events and relationships are from ourselves, our egos. Like clouds moving across the sky, we see in them what we will. We come to understand how we created the shapes we see in the clouds. But that deep blue sky in the background, upon which the clouds play and pass, by which the clouds are visible and take magnificent form, how can we feel less than pure peace and love towards the backdrop?

So, I understand that all of my reactions are just that. And I'm not angry anymore at myself. Better to forgive myself and others continuously, and don't take life so seriously.

As my ego cracks open, I don't need to hold onto those feelings gently placed in the breadbasket. For how greatly I am loved by the One so outshines those little things.

Compared to the love of Divine Grace, there is nothing else.

I am in the Grace of the One right now. I have always been in God's Grace, evident now by the values and beliefs I've always selected. And by my ability to love. Where did I get all this love from? I have been poured upon by the One.

There is nothing else I have to do or not do. Simply drop my luggage at the door, enfold my ego, my smaller self, and offer it up at the door of transformation. I don't need to wait until I'm spiritual someday. The time is now.

The book *The Secret* became famous today, when Oprah Winfrey hosted a show with its author and a panel of the writers from the book. Although not a secret to many, for "as a man thinketh... so is he" has been an axiom for ages. And not quite the whole picture, because the universe should get more credit for creativity, but *The Secret* will get the masses to begin thinking about their thinking. There's probably a fancy scientific name for that, but I'll call it self-awareness. Noticing one's thoughts and feelings, what causes them, and what to do to change them to help create a better life, is bound to raise consciousness. It's a great day for mankind!

When Oprah's guests discussed the power of attraction from *The Secret*, I thought, there is more positive energy on the way! People will have hope that they can change and create a better world. But then I watched people struggle with it. Some felt guilty or ignorant for not having lived in awareness sooner. For years they hadn't watched and controlled their thoughts, feelings and behavior. So they toss out the book as hogwash, drop the idea of controlling their own life, and go back to floating adrift as a victim of circumstances. But they needn't. When you wake up from a dream, you don't judge the dream. Maybe see what you can learn from it. Their past was just a dream to their present aware Self. They did the best they could with what they knew at the time. They can continue living in their limited mind, their prison, or rejoice in a new adventure of becoming, where the mind is a playground. Try some of this stuff, and see what happens!

My Ego - My Best Friend

"I am" may be the most significant phrase governing historical manifestation, where anything can be put after those words, but "I am not" seems more appropriate now. I already knew that I am not my body or brain, not what I have, what I do, or what others think of me. And now, knowing that I am not the one in the drama, with just a few minor character traits to tweak before reaching imagined perfection, is also a relief.

So, if "I am not" this, that and the other, while the layers of the onion are peeled away, why, I have made a good soup! Curiously, there is nothing in the center of the onion resembling the onion.

Truly believing I am not my ego is like getting a free train ticket to anywhere, from my ego! It is letting me go, with its best wishes, no tricks up its sleeves this time. It has made great strides, and I love it for that. It was indispensable for maneuvering me through lessons in my life. It's been my best friend.

Releasing me from its bonds is its own death sentence, but it is not afraid anymore. It knows what's best for it and me. It will always have a part in the Divine Show, as a playful and attentive student. Behind the curtain it has been paid well.

Perhaps it rests, too, when I board that train.

The ego starts moving out when your non-effort begins. (Although "begins" sounds like effort!) When you just don't care enough to be or do anything, it's out of a job. Its time is up. You both say goodbye, and que será será. You don't need each other anymore.

And while it dissolves, like the skilled magician it has been, you are set free.

It admits that You made it up. You are the better magician, but a comrade to the end.

45

Facing Fear

The birds hop along the fence from the tree to the bird feeder. Cautious, skittish, sometimes they fly back to the tree before they arrive at the feeder at the far end of the fence. Although they are afraid to continue, and think the tree is a safe haven, they might get something different than they expect. A black cat occasionally sneaks into the tree. A hungry cat.

I dreamed the other night, that I was headed home late from walking, and it was almost dark. I would usually go down a busy county road, but figuring it would be dark and some unsavory person might get me, I decided to take a different route, down a quiet street where I could loop around and come up by my home.

Turns out, a river was at the bottom of the hill, and I'd have to swim along the edge a ways before cutting up toward my place. So I jumped in, but it was faster than it looked, and perhaps rapids were ahead, so I got back up on the bank and had to crawl up a slippery muddy hill. I would now have to head through bushes up to the original detour, and walk the county road, after all.

In running away from imagined danger, I had chosen a path with real and worse danger, and would have to face my fears all over again.

So, who knows where danger lies. For the birds, is it out in the open as prey to hawks at the feeder, or in the tree?

I had spent a lot of time in my dream getting back to the same point, being diverted by fear. The birds take a long time to get to the food to eat. I think facing our fears gets us through life faster and in a more confident manner. Although nothing is wrong with the long way around.

What You Don't Know

Sometimes I greet people, "Tell me what you know." They usually respond, "Not much." This exchange is founded on the belief that the more you know, the better. We have a desire and even a need to know. But sometimes, what you don't know, equally defines a good life.

A miniature Dachshund (weenie dog) runs out and barks at us every day on our walk. Such a small dog, it's comical! It apparently never looked in a mirror, and thinks it's a humongous, intimidating dog.

Also, it protectively guards the family's four pet rabbits that run loose now and then in the backyard. It sits near them and watches them, like a sheep dog. It doesn't know Dachshunds were bred to hunt rabbits, thus the long pointed snouts and the digging claws. No one ever told it!

We don't need to know everything to be happy. We may be less happy if we knew more. Some people in remote third world countries are content to live simply, and not assimilate the materialistic American lifestyle. They don't know any different. Most people with developmental disabilities like Down's Syndrome are simple minded and extremely happy. And my favorite example, the more information we gain from the news, the more we have to worry about.

Watch nature, and there's always something to learn, even from a silly weenie dog!

Whatever path I'm on, I'm on it. Good thing I love walking!

The Balance of Opposites

If a principle/law like the law of attraction worked for everyone, how would this affect our world of polarity? Can it all become positive? Assume even criminals and psychopaths wanted to be better and seek their highest good. If people watch and improve their thoughts, words and deeds, a higher consciousness is achieved. At what point, in a world of opposites, are other laws (principles) affected by a change - increase or decrease - in one law? Does this manifestation of life on earth - the balance of opposites - change, and to what?

Bear in mind, this may never happen on this earth before we destroy it, but theoretically, it could. And it must be happening somewhere in other dimensions.

Is the Law of Positive Thinking Ever Negative?

One person's reaction to the law of attraction or positive thinking as expressed in *The Secret,* "It's not possible for everyone, depending on what country or the conditions in which you live. If you live in a war-torn country or have a serious health problem, although miracles can be created in some lives, many people will continue to be unsuccessful in making better lives." So for them, *The Secret*'s positive thinking is useless, perhaps even negative, if it provides false hope. Critics of the law of attraction say it is more for those already in situations with opportunity available, like in the USA. It's an elitist philosophy.

And aren't some doomed to fail, to carry out the Principle (Law) of Polarity, or their own soul's path? In a universe of opposites, it seems a paradox that we must try to raise our consciousness, knowing that for "Reality" to exist, many are going to struggle and fail.

I can see both sides to this argument, but know they are somehow united in only one truth. What is that truth?

Song of Grace

I am in the grace of the One right now,
I am in the grace of the One.
I have always been in the grace of the One,
in the grace of the One true love.
I've wanted a reason to give up the search,
and now that the seeker's been found,
by my very Self,
by the One true love,
by the grace of the One in the now.

Behind the Curtain

I opened the bedroom drapes, then lay back in bed to watch the rising sun. It was cloudy - the sun was hazy. *Isn't that just like life?* I thought. It can't come in until we open the curtain, and then the light may be dim.

The first time we open the curtain on the stage of life, we play both audience and actor, and either enjoy or tolerate the show, depending on the jest of the play, our mood and our expectations. But what we really want to know, after hours of diligent observation and participation, is: what transpires *behind* stage?

Who adjusts the lighting, creates the scenery, and decides the stage directions for the actors?

So, we go to the director and discuss the action on stage and the subtle control behind the stage and get the bigger picture, but implore: "what does it all mean?"

Then, when we understand much, we seek the playwright, asking: "with my knowledge, can I become the director now?"

The Playwright, who has the dream and inspiration for the play, ordains:

"First, know the Knower."

I wonder if It is the same One who creates *this* story you are reading.

We'll find out, if we relentlessly meet the hazy dawn, as it burns away to reveal the radiance.

First Feelings of Grace

I feel grace in the Oneness of a circle of friends, in a hug, when I give or receive a kindness, when I witness a kindness. Wherever true love is expressed, I feel the tingle of God's love, which is grace.

I am a brimming reservoir, pouring love from the Divine, as I am filled again and again. I am swimming in this flow, which is grace, like a fish in water. The touch of God, of being a vessel and conduit, is grace. It saturates my pores. There is no part of me untouched by love.

At sunrise, I'll open the curtain and trust the new day, leave my luggage at the gateway, enter the realm of the sacred fire, the heart of creation, and be burned unrecognizable.

There is nothing else to do, really. Others can do it. I am not indispensable! You and I are no less and no other than All That Is.

But, if I am to remain a doer still, if this is the will of the All, so be it, joyfully.

For I'll remember, I am so beloved, that my essence was and will eternally be merged with the One, joined with the Lover of Life.

Grace comes when we surrender to life, accept the whole enchilada, AS IS. By grace we experience a new love and oneness with life Itself. Oneness with others we've felt, but oneness with life Itself - AS IS - is a new Love.

The Way of the Tao (which tries to point, then get out of its own way) is to trust in nature and natural laws. Simply relish the *Is*-ness of life, the existence of life, Being dancing as us, our beings.

When opposites merge, joined in the dance of Life and creation, we see both sides to every story. The cup is both half-full and half-empty, and neither half-full nor half-empty. It's just a glass of delicious water for us to quench our thirst.

A silly rhyme from childhood goes: "Yours is not to question why, yours is just to do or die." Reverend Pope would say: "Yours is not to question why, yours is just to do or *not do*, and die." Either be doers, or don't! Either live, or die. But the Grace of the Divine is yours at any point in the universe, because IT IS YOU.

Everything is always in Divine Order (where I Am meandering on my path with Life), so at any time I can say:

"I am in my right and perfect place, now."

"It is what It is, and It's All that there is" were the only words you could hear from the hippy minister with a tattooed dolphin on his neck, who forgot to use the microphone at my son's wedding. Perhaps that was enough of a blessing.

I feel like a giddy child going on an adventure, where I trust my guide, and I know that nothing short of spectacular will be the results of the journey. Or going on a treasure hunt, where you already have the prize but you keep playing just for the fun of it.

I loved the part in the movie *Contact,* where Jody Foster is going through a wormhole of consciousness, encompassed in visceral swirling energy and beauty, and she just keeps repeating: "No words, no words, no words, no words," because she witnesses eternal nature (meaning without psychological time).

After a wonderful guided meditation at Unity worship one Sunday, I thought: "We can all go home now. Don't need any talk or message. There is nothing else to do or not do. God loves us exactly how we are, at this moment. Really, nothing to say. This is it. Oh, wait a minute. We are home!"

The Answer to All Questions

One Saturday night, I wrote in my journal: "Since we live in a world of opposites, it seems the law of attraction and the law of polarity end up in a face-off. For "reality" to exist as we know it, aren't different levels of consciousness necessary? Aren't some doomed to fail?

But the next day at church, I received the answer to this and other questions left unanswered in my consciousness: "It doesn't matter. It's all in Divine Order. Trust the Process."

And it makes sense. I watched a program on Doomsday, the top 10 threats to mankind's annihilation. The earth is overdue for a super volcano or a meteor, then we've got the bomb, germ warfare, and global warming. Each possible threat was discussed to scare the viewers, but instead of fear, I felt increasingly cozy and safe. Because I realized that we are living only by grace, and in grace, all the time! The Grace of Divine Order. Life is all being worked out for our highest good. If those things were going to annihilate earth, they would have done so already. We are in a protected mode, a higher order, a nourishing consciousness.

Love is the answer to every question. Divine Order is a reflection of universal love.

Be still and know that I am God.
Be still and know that I am.
Be still and know that I.
Be still and know that.
Be still and know.
Be still and.
Be still.
Be.

Love is like a boomerang. You give it out and it comes back in full force and hits you in the head. So much love was shared at the ceremony tonight, I'm giddy, almost silly. Being hit too much by the boomerang!

It's good to know our reverend is human! His squaring up about the downside of his day, saying or not saying the "right" or "wrong" thing, brought his own point exactly home to rest: that we are all doing the best we can, that we are all accepted "as is" under the wings of Grace, and are loved exactly as we are.

Why do you think the *Da Vinci Code* was so popular? People want to believe Jesus was human and had relationships, which we know have highs and lows. If he could still stay connected to God, Grace still flowed into and through Him, then what does that say for you and I?

That even in our pain and suffering of the human condition, we are still one with the Source of Grace. Once it begins to shine, the Christ Mind is hard to squelch.

Doing the Best We Can

It was difficult for many at the last gathering to admit that President Bush is doing the best he can. How about a murderer or rapist, are they doing their best? But the statement is either true or not, that we are all doing the best we can. Take a crooked politician. He knows he's being crooked. Is this the best he can do? In our view, no! Maybe later in his life or earlier in his life he would have a different perspective and not commit the acts he does in the present. But in any given moment, say his name is Jerry, he is expressing his *Jerry*-ness the best way he knows how. He may feel he is doing wrong or not, feel crooked - or not. But either way, it's all he is capable of doing at the moment, all he has the heart, intelligence, or moral responsibility to act upon, all the integrity he can muster. He may not be running on all cylinders.

This holds true for someone having an abortion, a terrorist, a rapist, an abusive parent or spouse, a thief, or a crooked politician. They certainly have room to grow and change and come into harmony and right action with others, but it's all they've got at the moment. It's like a golf handicap, but in life. Hopefully, they will improve.

Besides, the law of polarity supplies the learning field. If all acted perfectly, there'd be no room for anyone to grow or learn, and the world would cease as we know it.

Grace at Dawn

I watched the sunrise yesterday with two birds. They sat perched on the top branch of a tree. Other birds went about their business already, hopping and chattering inside a different tree. For fifteen minutes, as the sun rose, I caught every nuance of radiant light engulfing the clouds. Those two birds also faced the sun, quiet, not communing with each other, exposed, watching, receiving. They were focused on the dawn, and not each other.

Always looking to nature for pointers, "How nice," I thought, "two birds, together, enjoying nature, how it used to be with my partner. It means peaceful relationships are possible. A joining of my soul to another. Maybe a good omen."

Today, when I watched the sunrise, only one bird sat there alone and only lingered a while before flying high into the sky. "Perhaps it was my timing," I thought. "Maybe there were two earlier, or will be later. Maybe a whole group brought in the dawn. I just missed it."

But deep inside, I knew. We are all that solitary bird. At the last dawn, we shall fly into the sky, alone, hopefully embodied in peace, love and joy. Leaving in grace as we lived in grace and were born by grace. Departing back into the Oneness. For there is only One, and when stripped of our ego, we are that One.

The paradox is: when we are totally alone, crossing the line at our time of transition from this life, we feel like no one, and lonely. But in an instant, we are the One And Only, the All, which is everywhere and everyone. So the solitary bird is an illusion.

A Walk With My Higher Self

My walk around the block this morning was surrealistic. Heading out my door, the thought crossed my mind: "I'll walk around the block and not judge all the trashy places." Condemned shacks and carefully attended homes are side-by-side in my neighborhood. I usually judge each place as I go, like a Christmas yard-decorating contest. "Too many cars in the yard. Cracking cement. Gorgeous green lawn. Nice new fence."

I made it to the first neighbor. "That plastic bag is still hanging in the tree," I thought. The next house, "plum colored tree. Such green grass." I was aware as I walked, that I felt better noticing beauty and improvements, and directed my attention only to such places, ignoring and hence not judging the junky places. What a difference I was feeling as I walked in this manner, deciding where to focus. *I'm learning something about selecting a viewpoint!* I thought excitedly.

Lessons began emerging as I activated my conscious attention. I walked by a dense line of pine trees. The original owner of the property planted them too close together. Half of each tree was unformed as it tucked inside the tree next to it. This is how it is in relationships, I thought. When individuals grow into their fuller selves, they must watch they are not planted too close to be in each other's shade, or they don't develop half of their branches.

Next, was a bumper sticker on a truck: PAIN IS WEAKNESS LEAVING THE BODY. This was coincidentally the logo of my son's unit in the Coast Guard. I reflected on how this is true for spiritual growth as well. Growing creates birthing pains of our spirits, of our awakening hearts. Thankfully, always followed by the relief of Grace. Pain is weakness leaving, making room for a stronger self.

Then I walked past a group of brilliant fuchsia fruit trees. That intense color lasts only a short while, I realized. If I had those trees in my yard I'd be gazing at them and appreciating them every day. Such beauty! Life is like that, I thought. So short is our particular road. Maybe I should relish the beauty of life every day, knowing its color is fading.

Finally, the last few days I noticed and felt bad for a big cactus that someone had set aside when they landscaped. Its roots lay exposed to the summer sun, a sure death sentence. But today I saw, that being exposed was a blessing. It had received a little drink from the rain last night. Other nearby cactus had roots too far in the ground to benefit from the sprinkling. So, the lesson? Showing our vulnerability (roots) can be nourishing. As I paused, a neighbor from across the street came over and said she had asked the owners if she could have the cactus, they'd consented, and she would plant it tomorrow. Hooray!

"So, enough already!" I told myself. "I've got to quit paying attention. Too many lessons!" Maybe by suspending judgment and asking to see what I could learn, my spirit or higher self had brought me all these lessons. It was definitely a different experience that day on my usually boring walk.

Today, on my walk, I saw a bumper sticker:

TRUTH
SOUL
AMOR

It's what I've been trying to point at!

At dawn this morning, the single bird flew into the treetop again. I felt content that it was alone today. But then another bird flew in, distracted it, they perched only a minute, and then flew away, missing the quiet of the rising sun. From my side of the window, I was peaceful this morning. No heart on fire. No words racing to get on paper. A jet was passing over leaving a cherry line across the sky. The trail of a dawnrider, I thought. Like me.

I am a windstar
I am a dawnrider
I am the portal.
Although a windstar and a dawnrider need an "I am",
The Portal does not.

Horrific winds buffeted our boat, and we hid inside a boulder cave on the lake to wait it out. My clutching fingers left imprints on the aluminum dashboard. With only a few hours of daylight left and miles to travel, we fearfully headed back out into the oceanic waves. Coming around a corner, to our great surprise, a guy on a surfboard with a sail was flying across the crests of the waves. The windsurfer was fearless, at the height of his sport, in a flow of pure happiness. While I'd been clinging for dear life to the dashboard of my boat in a hellish panic, he was in heaven. Climbing the ladder of consciousness, we must be like the windsurfer. Simply hold on.

Was it a coincidence? At home all morning, writing about going with the flow of the wind, I finally emerged and drove to the store. On the rear of the car in front of me was an emblem - WINDSTAR. I don't usually read car emblems, but it seemed a message from the universe that I was on track, becoming the windstar I had thought about that morning.

April 2007

YOU HAVE TO BE GOING SOMEWHERE TO GET LOST, the sign said.

(As you can tell by now, some signs speak to me!)

I read this two ways. If you don't get off your butt and go somewhere, of course you'll never get lost. You're not doing anything.

OR

If you just travel along on the journey of life, no concrete destination, you won't ever be lost since you are exactly where you are. So, if I get lost going from point A to point B in my life, it won't be for long, because I'll realize I'm never really lost, but on the correct path. I'm not going somewhere, because I'm always here.

Spirituality is not a mantle you pick up and cover yourself with, or examine the threads of the cloak and say, "I'll wear that when I'm older, maybe 50 or 60, but it's not for me right now." You are a spiritual being by your very nature. There's no way you can't be. There is no choice. Spiritual consciousness-energy-matter is in all space and all things. There is nowhere it is not. And that includes you! Since there is nowhere to hide from yourself, once you are aware that you are aware, you might want to connect to the bigger picture, the bigger Self that you are.

HaPPILy StuCk iN tHe MuD
(In My Present Level of Consciousness)

Why would I want to go home, when the party's just begun?

Would the One And Only really want all Its pieces back, if It gave them away in the first place?

Why is I AM up at three in the morning writing, if the rules of my life are already written?

Do I want to wake up and smell the coffee if the coffee's bad for me? Or maybe bad for "I"? Or even IT? What would IT do with all the pieces, anyway?

And finally, and of gravest consideration, when did pronouns get so important?

If the answer to every question is maybe yes and maybe no, why bother to ask questions?

Exactly!

Well. Since consciousness Itself is ever expanding,
you'll never catch up!

So you might as well take off your running shoes
and stay for the party!

I see no reason to pack my bags until I'm evicted.

The billboard suggested: ELEVATE YOUR LIFE. Of course, it meant to buy real estate near the sign, Flagstaff, Arizona, which is 7000 feet high. But I took it as a reminder to seek the higher life.

If life is like riding a bucking bronco, you can ride it well, win some prizes along the way, but always end up on the floor on your knees. Maybe I just won't bother with the ride, but get on my knees to begin with.

I asked Ram Tzu: "Why would I want to go home, when the party's just begun?"

Meaning that my life is full of joy, love, harmony, peace, all a person could want. And *going home* to God in spirit is a merging Oneness, where perhaps none of this, or even I, exist. Seems like a duty to go, not a choice.

Ram Tzu replied: "Perhaps the party is at your house."

I laughed aloud at his perfect answer.

I have always liked the Bob Seger song *Against the Wind*. To me the act of running against the wind symbolized strong and free individuals standing against society and all odds. Trying to keep our spirits high and intact, the wind being the brainwashing pouring on us from society, telling us what to do and how to think, and that the values of the status quo were normal.

Some years later, I see the wind differently. Other people (not me, of course) were going against the wind, fighting the rising, awakening Spirit that called them to live a spiritual life. They refused to go with the wind or flow of their spiritual nature, fighting their own personal best interests in this scenario, not society as in the first example. But until I heard that song by chance (yeah, right) today, I didn't figure out the message that was for me.

The other night, I wrote about being a windstar and about the windsurfer, how rising in consciousness you must just hold on in the wind and enjoy the ride. So it hits me. *I'm* the one fighting the flow of the spirit, of nature, of Divine Order, wanting to gently push me along in Its breezes. *I* need to let go. If the angels can fly because they take themselves lightly, I need to take myself less seriously, pop the balloons of my ideas, thoughts, habits and plans, and be more formless. Without all that luggage and airbags, maybe I'll be easier to push. And be a real windstar.

Cold Feet

If the yearning of our spirits to go *Home* is a true choice, do we obliviously merge with God because we love that energy the most, or stay to love humanity in the muck and mire?

I can't imagine it would be a choice between loving God or loving humanity, since loving God includes loving humanity, and loving humanity *is* loving God.

It seems that beings in a non-dualistic atmosphere would have no shape to their existence, no individuality, not beings in any concrete sense of the word. Non-being beings. If they were One with God/Consciousness, they wouldn't be "they" being anything.

And since they would *BE* Love, they wouldn't need it or want it. Living on the earth we can be love, but we also need love. If the world was not needy of love, it would be perfect, and not reality as we know it. The world would either cease existence or be heaven on earth! Every thing's possible. Perhaps more than one scenario is going on in more than one dimension, simultaneously!

Beyond my individuality and ego, a tad of Pure Consciousness is playing as me, truly lost in that role. If I acknowledge and release It to do as It wishes, in fact, hand It the reins, would It not by nature begin loving humanity where It stood, perhaps with more power and full of Grace and wisdom? So, If I am It unfolding, I am the door by which Divine Spirit enters, rolls up Its sleeves and gets to work. It would be compelled to be all It can be, and to love others. And if that is what I am already doing, am I already It, materialized through the door?

I guess what I'm saying is that, if this world and life on this planet matters at all, if God can use me here, isn't that better than my being pure bliss somewhere beyond time and space?

But, if there were really a choice to go *Home*, and I wouldn't feel selfish, or that I'd not done my best to help humanity, which road would I take?

Funny, you spend 50 years learning stuff (great knowledge), then 20 trying to unlearn it. The only reason you might be able to unlearn 50 years in 20 is that you're more aware the last 20 years.

Easter

My first realization this morning is that I'm learning lessons and unlearning lessons at the same time. So I hope things don't get mixed up! If they do, I'll just catch them the next time they come around. Or not!

I was in a dream state, not asleep and not awake. I'd peeked a few moments at the rising sun, said "Thanks!" climbed back in bed and dozed.

In this waking dream, I was at a crowded gathering, when a boy from India came up to me and offered me a single white rose. As I reached for it he quietly spoke: "You can pass it on." It was so realistic; he had a small scar above his left eye. I gave him a hug, which we together filled to overflowing with enormous energy and love.

When I woke, I felt something special had happened, but had no idea what. When I told my reverend about it, I was choked up. He said it symbolized purity and divine love. I asked a teacher of Indian spirituality (they call it Consciousness) and he said it meant I was loved very much. That it coincided with Easter is interesting. It was the only such dream I have ever had.

Need to Let Go

I need to let go, now. I've done the best I can, and all I can toward my spiritual growth. If the Grace of the Divine, the Eternal Love of the One Presence would rain on me, and surge from within, I could transcend the limitations of myself and resurrect to the One I am meant to be. But not by my hand will this fruit be grown.

So until the rain comes to the desert, it lacks blooms, yet is full of possibility and expectancy of fruition.

Soon, I will even give up the hope and need to let go. I'll go back to my little life, where I've been waiting for years, unbeknownst to my higher Self, to be born again by Grace.

Yours Truly,
Not-so-happily-stuck-in-the-mud

Rise & Fall

Who says the One And Only doesn't have a sense of humor. We have been programmed (if everything is always in Divine Order) to build up our egos for 50 years, and then try and tear them down, dismantle them over the next 10, or quicker if possible, to reap the benefits of greater consciousness, thereby fulfilling our humanity.

It's like encouraging your children to build a wonderful sand castle or block tower, putting their full potential to work, then coming along and knocking it down, or chuckling when the waves come for the castle.

But we finally learn that building only exists because destroying allowed the bare essence to be available. We feel the rise and fall of existence in the rise and fall of ourselves.

MY LIFE IS MY ALTAR.

The Hawk

This morning at sunrise, a solitary bird joined me in honoring the day. Perched in the treetop, perhaps it didn't know a hungry hawk had just swooshed through, posed on the fence by the bird feeder, and then continued its hunt. The other birds were still in the dense bushes chirping about their near death experience.

But perhaps the solitary bird knew, and just didn't care. Soon other birds came out and perched in the tops of the tree, greeting the sun in silence, the only few minutes of quiet in their usually chatty, busy lives.

So we were a sacred gathering. None of us caring that the hawk comes for the dawnriders. And we are ready to go.

Who's in Control?

If everything is always in Divine Order, I feel rather like a moth in the matrix, where all end up in the flaming light. I like options, menus for everything. If my choices aren't my choices, on the one hand it's comforting that I'm not going through a maze. And I can just do my best.

"Divine Order" hints of fate. But I don't mind being a puppet; I have a great play I'm in. I just hope I can relinquish control and by Grace become more self-less. It would make life easier.

But since fate includes chaos, even my rebellion would be sanctioned in the grand scheme of things. If all parts and scenarios are acceptable, all outcomes approved, it helps me give up personal will, because there wouldn't be any anyway.

So I walk whatever path rises to meet me, wondering, who's doing the walking?

May 2007

Climbing the Ladder of Consciousness:
rising above the level of the heart

With deepest respect
the way to God
is wherever my feet are.
God loves me, and there is nothing I can do
or not do about it.
My path is
to sit still and let Him!

I'm like a rolling stone,
learning, learning knowledge, seeking, chasing ideas.
But a rolling stone gathers no moss.
I want to sit and grow moss around my feet.

With final illumination you will say, "I'm not in Kansas anymore!"
Isn't that where you've always wanted to go back to? Kansas?
Your home, your dream, love, joy, peace, harmony.
Why would you want to leave that?
Why do you want to go back?
Because we are adventurous travelers?
I still prefer the thought of moss to netti-netti.

Where I'm at in spirituality: I want to have my cake and eat it too.
Be a part of life. I want the love, joy, and peace.
Those that seek pure consciousness are where there is no cake.

I can't look at the sun, it's too bright.
But those stages of the dawn heralding It,
full of love, joy and peace,
those I'll continue to watch.
Why was Icarus flying into the sun, anyway?
Are we only moths?

I enjoy being the watcher,
and I love to love.
Why would I want enlightenment
when life is so good as it is?
If nirvana is no mind,
how much life do you feel?
I relish not wanting, but not choosing?
Pure consciousness would have no selection.

I love the love of God in your soul.
I love the love of God in my soul.
This is heart to heart. Isn't this the supreme lesson and reward?

Love, God, soul, the last words I'm holding onto. Tightly.

I put my hands over my heart.
"I'm not giving up my heart!"
I wept.
Then, I realized, it's not my heart, it's a borrowing.
A part of the One, the One And Only Itself.
I touched my heart gently.
I am a pedestal for the Heart of God.
But why was I so sad?
It's still my ego, thinking something is mine!
But it's not *my* loving heart, no matter what the songs say.
And there is also a deep joy behind the tears.

On moving up the chart,
I wanted to take my heart,
but I know it's there waiting for me at the top,
when I return my part.

The last leg of my spiritual journey,
is like being in my bed, so warm and comfy.
I don't want to get up.
But I guess I will!
You said it didn't matter if the doer does or not,
it's all being worked out as we go.
So I'll just stay in bed. Wait a minute. I have to go pee!
But I prefer to lay in bed and listen to my heartbeat.

It seems selfish to seek enlightenment, higher consciousness, for your own sake, once you reach the level of the heart. In a dualistic world, the level of love is the focus to create a better world. Why do you want to go to your enlightenment anytime soon? You won't be there to celebrate your crowning achievement! Although it might not matter what you do or don't do, being a Self-seeking organism that needs soul gratification still reeks of effort and ego. Better to let the higher levels of consciousness seek you. But I understand. I, too, am like a kite on a breezy day. Please tie some weights on my feet!

In Love

Oh my gosh. No. Oh my God. It dawned on me driving home Tuesday night, that something my teacher uttered quietly amidst all the caring advice was the truest. "You are in love."

My heart leaped when I realized. Yes. I am in love! That explains it. And with the One And Only, no less. I can surrender now. Because I know my best interests will always be at heart. What a great adventure of joining this will be.

I don't need maps or directions to my God. No steps to follow or ladder to climb to higher consciousness. The One And Only is relentlessly wedged in my heart.

And I want that my will is God's will, because who knows best. And He/She would never reduce me to a puppet, nor take me against my will. So my heart feels safe, free, and given freely, at last.

The sun is always shining, we're just not aware of it. Every dawn, it seems the dark gives birth to the light of the rising sun. But that's our limited perspective, the point of view from which we see. Actually, the sun is always shining. And so it is with the dark days of our lives. The light is always there, we just catch and ride the next rotation to greet it. As the sun is our source of life on this planet, the Light of Forever always holds our soul.

"Return to me, and I will return to you," I repeated. "Return to me, and I will return to you." The downpour of Grace over the last few months had subsided. How had I lost the connection? Or had I assimilated that quickening - temperature rising, heart open, mind clear.

Returning to Source sounds like I need to travel somewhere. And since I feel I have absolutely nowhere to go, maybe I'm already "there"... and just don't know it yet. The lyrics of a song go, "There's nowhere to go, but there's miles and miles of road."

So my heart lays still and steadfast, waiting for the returning, for the joining. I'm done traveling, done with the "there" and the "here", just done.

So how can I return, when there are no steps?

And when any direction is moving away, off-center?

Unless my center is everywhere, and no matter what I do - it is a returning.

June and July 2007

I live in my RV, which borders an apple orchard. Every morning before dawn, a robin does revelry at the top of its lungs. Soon another bird, then another joins in. No gentle chirping or chattering. That comes later. They all exclaim in the loudest bird sound, celebrating:

"It's a new day! The sun is rising!"

For me, the joy is that they do it every dawn, without fail.

For them, the joy is that each morning they rally so enthusiastically, it seems to be a brand new and totally fulfilling ritual. Every day is like the first time.

It is much like a part of our story, you and I.

We are the rabble-rousers, the first and loudest birds. And as we join in the celebration of single heart and no mind, and sing together and worship the dawn of a new day, we are complete in that moment. For each dawn comes closer and closer together, heralding the coming of the final dawn.

To include him at the gathering, I asked a quiet elderly gentleman who pushed a walker: "So, how do you handle all this beauty?" We live in the White Mountains of Arizona.

"I just breathe deeply, and wait to see what tomorrow brings."

"That's it!" I replied. "It's all so simple. Now, if I could just get the little thoughts, the chattering pushed aside. And really do that." Our hearts smiled, the man, his wife and I.

Instant Life

Reverend Brooks talked about instant Life. "There is instant oatmeal, instant messaging, and instant gratification. So I'm here today to tell you about instant life." Our connection to God is in the moment, in the blink of an eye. If He/She is nearer to us than our breath, we can be in the now at any moment, connected. This is instant Life.

We're satiated with It. Dining unawares, we are always hooked up to our Lifeline. But only in the present moment. Never the past or future. Just NOW. And NOW, again. And yet again, in *this* instant.

Do a little exercise: Relax a few minutes, breathe deeply, and watch your breathing. Then say to yourself: "What will my next thought be?" Be extremely watchful. Wait to see what comes into your mind. In Eckhart Tolle's *The Power of Now,* he says to pretend your awareness is like a cat waiting for a mouse to come out of its hole, and you are ready to pounce on the thought.

You will create a gap in psychological time between past and future. This awareness is a presence - your spirit or consciousness and the Eternal Field together - connected outside of psychological time. This is the dimension of eternity, where you meet the Divine, by whatever name or image you choose.

So take time every day - for instant Life!

August & September 2007

I have fewer and fewer questions, when the answer is: "Mystery."
And more and more light when the universe responds: "I will show you."

As I bathe in the morning light through my window pane, there are no questions and answers, only warmth and joy, as my inner and the outer light connect and reflect rainbow sparks.

We are satiated with God's love. Do we know it? We are swimming in God's abundance. Do we cling to the shore? Thinking of yesterday, dreaming of tomorrow, do we miss the dance right NOW?

Remember, the choice is between slavery and the unknown. Slavery to my thoughts, emotions, status quo way of life, the old me, or leaping into the dark. Mankind must make that leap now or perish. But our egos use fear to hold us plodding to the current, known course, a reign of control with safe and limited thinking. If only we could realize, the choice isn't between slavery or the unknown, but slavery or *freedom.* And in that freedom is a light, a brilliant light of which we are all One. No more darkness!

Birthing a New Consciousness

Lately, I actually feel like some part of me has ascended from this life, and left the shell to finish duties. On my walks the last two days I was SO tired, I had to concentrate - left foot, right foot - to get started. I walk in a daze, where nothing fazes my consciousness. I am calm, and in the stillness, feel an intense oneness with a peaceful vibration.

Then BAM! I'm thrown back to earth again. I know I'm not going crazy. All I know, really, is that I love God and trust the outcome.

I am trying to remember to breathe. Fortunately, I am not too entrenched or attached to the world anymore, so the labor of birthing my new consciousness is not too painful.

October 2007

Dream ~

In some unknown twilight zone nightclub lounge, I was riding a mechanical bull for the first time. I rode it for 15 minutes without falling, in a lace skirt, squeezing my knees tightly and holding its head with my hands. It finally tired and lay down on its side. People left. The bull was real, and said it had a hard day the day before on some outing. I felt compassion. Then it got the strength to do a few more minutes of bucking, the best yet, and it was a great finish to my ride. I was trying to call someone back to see how good I could ride even when the bull was giving such stupendous effort. I was really in tune, also giving my all, in flow with the bucking. We were both having a good time, doing our best, comrades to the end. Of course, I was the champion.

I woke up feeling: it takes 2 to do the show, to prove oneself. The bull and I were joined in this ceremony. I felt this was a dream about duality.

107

Be Thankful for Being

I am so thankful, that when people send me Thank-You cards, I want to send them one back. Maybe I'll create a new line of Thank-You cards saying: "Thank you for thanking me. It made my day complete."

When I got home one day and checked my answering machine, someone had left a message: "Thanks for the birthday song you left on my voicemail." I fought the urge to call right back and thank them for calling and thanking me. A thankful heart, you see, goes on and on!

Inner Peace is Knowing You're Right Where You're Supposed to Be

On a 3 week "vacation", my brother was in the San Diego fires, my daughter had an auto accident, and friends went to the hospital. Everyone's alive, thank God. But everyday, to keep peace and sanity, I sang a chant: "Thank you for this day, Spirit, thank you for this day."

Back home, on my way to church this morning (I almost didn't go but something was dragging me), I was thinking about someone I needed to forgive. It had been eight months, and I was tired of not being able to resolve this roadblock to my peace of mind and spiritual growth. While driving, I reflected, "I'm feeling slightly over the hump, and soon, I'll be able to get over it and get beyond it." When I arrived at Unity church, guess the first song we rose to sing? The one I'd been singing for 3 weeks: "Thank you for this day, Spirit, thank you for this day." The choir director randomly grabbed a few people out of the audience to come to the stage and lead, including me!

And guess what the Sunday message was on? Forgiveness! Coincidence? Synchronicity? It was all just what I needed to hear. The Universe is ready and willing to provide guidance. On a deeper level, it means all things are in order in my life, and I'm right where I'm supposed to be at the right moment. That in itself brings inner peace.

Perspectives are stances of our ego, and as we choose them they control our experience. If we don't like where we're at, we can look at it differently. If we create a different thought about it, our feelings will change, and emotions become happier and calmer. Our perspectives are not the same as our being. The whole web is the Being, but while perspectives are of our minds, Being has heart. If you doubt that It has heart, just tune your dial to The Divine Show; It's always hugging us.

Forgiveness

We can forgive 10 things and hold onto only 1, but that is the main situation requiring our forgiveness, so we can get on with life and our spiritual growth.

Non-forgiveness of others is a resentment we are attached to, have been holding onto, as a part of our story. But we can exchange the non-forgiveness for the truth. The truth is that the other person acted from their position, without especially trying to hurt us. Their act or words were about them, their story, not you in particular. Don't take it personally.

Forgiveness deals primarily with ourselves. It's like holding something rotten in a container in our hearts. Something rotten, that if replaced with the truth, the total *poor me* picture would dissolve.

We must forgive everyone and everything. It is much better to forgive in the present than to hold onto things that build up. We would have a smiling heart if we forgave as we went. Lighten up! Look at it as people testing our patience, our understanding, and our resolve to not react from emotion. And to see the drama of the play we're in as the elements that develop our character.

About the past. You would not be where you are today or who you are without the trials you've faced or suffering you've endured. It is the marrow grown in your bones. The most grace comes to those whose hearts have been cracked. It is the way God can enter. Except for your path to this moment, you would not be sitting here reading this book, hopefully being enlightened by the minute.

When we first forgive others, for they know not what they are doing, it's a noble act. "You have wronged me, but I am over it now, and I love you, anyway." Forgive sincerely, accepting their story as part of your own; understand them. Don't forgive others just to feel better and balance yourself; although good psychological reasons for forgiveness, it robs your soul of genuine contrition.

In the end, you face the harder task of forgiving yourself for taking so long to truly forgive, for carrying the extra baggage of resentment along on your soul's quest for peace and freedom. We can forgive ourselves during the momentum of forgiving others, because after all is said and done, we are united by the same story.

But, dare I say it; can we forgive the Universal Oneness for the hand we are dealt? Were we in cahoots? Did the person born to less than perfect circumstances in a war-torn country or to abusive parents have a secret pact with the Consciousness of Love to suffer so until awakened from the nightmare? Once awareness comes to such humble spirits, they blossom into individuals with enormous compassion and the ability to teach others of love and oneness. But wasn't there some other way to build integrity?

So, as we decide to choose forgiveness, now that we finally can, bringing happiness and peace, let's not waste another day on misery. Let us give our blessing to our past and our present; bless those who suffer, bless those who cause suffering, and bless those who witness suffering, including ourselves. Let us bless life, as everything that has happened to us and all past choices have somehow blessed us and brought us to this moment today.

The Silence of Knowing is the title of a song I just heard on the radio. "Knowing what?" you might ask. Nothing in particular. Just knowing. Those who know understand what I'm pointing toward.

Embracing the Wind was another song. "How can you embrace something you can't see or touch?" you could ask. By simply knowing its presence as a gentle breeze or violent nudging, feeling its energy, and wrapping your open heart and soul around its essence.

Other songs I just heard: *That's How Strong My Love Is (*for God or Life), and *There's Nowhere to Go, But There's Miles and Miles of Road.* (So I might as well stay put? Or, maybe any road is a fine choice for the sake of going?) The Universe is always trying to teach us or entertain us!

November 2007

If your chosen view of reality is that it's all flowers and bunnies, it's true (for you). Your view is as much a part of Reality as all views. Prime Creator also shares in your view, among other views. Whether it's God's view or your personal view, is the matter of the chicken or the egg coming first. It's all One story with different characters, perspectives and stances.

When I leave, my loves, you will have footprints to follow. But always make sure you know where you are. For the birds will eat the crumbs I leave behind.

Any attempt to name the Nameless already moves us one step farther away.

Truly free people celebrate diversity. They don't argue over the most correct view. They don't kill over political or religious ideology, or out of hate or revenge. If we are really one people, one humankind, if we kill, we are killing ourselves. If we hate, we are hating ourselves. On this tiny blue planet, we are intimately connected in our biological and evolutionary nature, even our electromagnetic fields and consciousness are connected. There is no way to get away from ourselves, our shadow selves are always there, so we must learn to love. This is the only choice for survival of the species.

We must love ourselves, and that includes everyone else. We really must love our enemies as ourselves, because they are ourselves. We learn to love- or we perish. It's that simple. Compassion or death.

We must love unconditionally, which means forgiving things and people as they happen. Don't save resentments to forgive down the road. Life is happening too fast, we are ascending as a human race, there is no time for holding on to much of anything except love.

"It's All Good" is Bad?

A philosophy teacher said: "People that believe it's all good are not very bright. I mean, look around. Their view is myopic. It-is-what-it-is."

Yikes! *It's All Good* is the basic premise of my personal beliefs. Yes, I know, beliefs are like picking out of the candy bins at the five-and-dime, "two red, one green, 3 peppermint, please." I guess we all hold fast that our beliefs are true, while trying to accept others with different beliefs, and relinquish our ability to judge everything. I respect all beliefs, especially those centered in the notion we are all One. Most beliefs tend to divide us; we even allow wars over beliefs.

The teacher is playing judge by stating that the concept *It's all good* is wrong. I respond that *his* concept is wrong, because of its exclusivity. (Okay, I'm judging! But watch how this paradox turns into a win-win perspective.) I get the feeling that deep down, the teacher feels that it *is* all good, but *his* perspective - *his* view of God (he uses the word consciousness) is what's all good.

I believe "It's All Good" and "It's All God" are the same statement. If it exists, It must be God, if all existence is God, then all existence is good.

I didn't hear him use the word *love* much, although he said we behave according to our nature, and while not condoning it, we accept it. This idea reeks of love! He says that homosexuals, murderers, child molesters and cheating husbands are just following their nature, they have no real authorship, so are not real doers. He says this is just the way it is, beyond our control. This kind of acceptance could only be unconditional love.

116

I don't buy that our nature is beyond our control. Surely, tendencies and nature exist. But my idea is that we are all doing the best we can, mustering all the integrity we are capable of at any moment, yet we are capable of summoning dormant authorship over our own lives.

He shows deep respect when he says we're no less than a part of the whole Universe, the functioning of totality, no less than all there is, and our hearts are kept beating and the stars held in the sky by this great web of existence we can feel. How is he not saying It's All Good when he says this? I know he's saying It's All God.

I say It's All Good, good and bad combined are good, the teacher's view and mine are both good, the whole shebang is good.

Some of the drama within may not be – but there's always potential leading to good, or right action drawing towards the light. Even in the worse case scenario, annihilation, Shiva energy displays creation/destruction as intimate partners, the ups and downs of ascending human evolution.

But there is always a glimmer of light that holds fast in the depths of the human soul. To decree "*It's all good* is myopic," the light seems to be too dim, hopeless. Even one heart blazing on fire with the love of God brings hope, and is contagious.

Walking the path of duality, where life is paradoxical and downright humorous, words get us nowhere. Good/not good, nature/divine nature, belief/control/no authorship. I mean, really. Isn't even this all good, because it is all God? Although It-is-what-it-is, that *Is*-ness, the Ground of Being, is definitely a loving Goodness – to imagine and put up with us!

117

December 2007

Since I decided to choose joy, I've been finding myself now and then noticing, *What is this feeling?* And it's joy!

I didn't have to have everything aligned, all ducks in a row... simply choose it.

We make things so complicated sometimes.

Even the Dove® candy wrappers I opened said, "Joy to... you," and "Joy is contagious."

The Gift

On my walk in the forest this morning, wearing a green fleece and red vest I've worn a few times lately, but today lacking any Christmas cheer whatsoever, a strange thing happened. I meandered along, daydreaming, and there in the middle of acres of pine trees, I "happened" to glance down and spot a green bead. Smaller than a baby pea, but a Christmas color green, it was in front of me on the path. I picked it up, like a child finding a treasure. I never pick things up. I walked a few more steps, and there was another bead – a red one – and I picked it up. Amazing. Not another bead in sight – I combed the area – not a one. So in my pocket now are two tiny beads, sent by…? My spirit, the Spirit, the Universe, the functioning of totality?

So you tell me there's no love or grace out there in the ethers, in every cell of everything. I am loved, It's All Good, and was given a little Christmas cheer from the Universe – of which I am now a more aware and grateful part, not just a mechanical part. So I will continue to shine my tiny light because that's all that's needed. Like a flickering firefly searching for others – wings of light join as we do the Dance.

And It is Good!

The Last Transmission

If you had one page to write to everyone you knew and people in general before you died, a last transmission so to speak, what would it say?

First, you would express love to everyone you cared about, and to those you think you should have cared about more. You'd convey love to all heroes of mankind. You'd gently speak love to your higher consciousness, your God-Self. And express universal love for Life in general, every one and every thing. You would solemnly feel love for the life pulsing in your veins, and understand its sacredness and eternal nature. If only you had known sooner that our spirits are woven in one power that beats all our hearts, one presence that lives all our lives and one flowing activity. For we are Life, and we go on and on and on.

Next, you would give thanks for this love of which we are a part and from which we are never separated. And thanks for the whole shebang: the good, the bad, the ugly, and the beautiful. All experiences from which you learned, all experiences to which you missed the point. All people. All blessings. Thankful for the opportunity of the journey.

Then, you would tell people to open their eyes, open their minds, open their hearts and open their souls. To laugh at our seriousness. To take care of the earth. To give your life away, in money, compassion, and time.

To remember, *you could die tomorrow.* So always be accountable, be present, be happy and at peace.

And remember your oneness with all other beings. We breathe the same air in and out, we move in the same field of energy. All our differences are only in meanings of words.

When it's all said and done, what means the most to each of us are these expressions. Would it not be the same for each of you reading this? And for everyone? Does this not prove our oneness even beyond a shadow of a doubt?

So, good life to my friends, those I met and those I didn't. And remember, as I love you with all my heart, if you continue to love and think of me, we are always connected. Life continues by the grace of this field of love.

January 2008

When you don't have to have an opinion about things, you are free of being judge and ruler of the universe, and joy can rise.

We are not here to absorb the energy of our surroundings, but to expel our
energy to our surroundings.
We are here to sparkle and sizzle with the vim, vigor and zeal of life
manifesting.
To deflect the energies swirling in our personal and universal field,
as we burst forth,
eject our inward side outward.
We propel our spirit,
we take a stand,
we stand on this holy ground as the life
as the good
as the love
of the eternal omnipotence.

To claim this space as a cosmonaut warrior for Divine energy,
on this spot I shall raise my flag.
My essence be born, my energy overflowing,
spewing from the Ground-of-All-Being onto this ground,
and from this very spot to make a portal for the Divine to follow.

And none of this be the doing of little-me, except the humble offering of an
opening for the Universe to come through and make a stand,
a saving Grace.

The Portal

I am an opening for God.
Where this point of me is,
God rests, moves, has Its being and spirit.

In the end, when it's only echoes and heartbeats,
I will still shout for Silence.

In the beginning was only one light in the darkness.
In the end will be only one light in the darkness...
will it be mine?

This Portal works both ways. My spirit lives on both sides. Fear not when you come to this threshold, for there is nowhere God is not. Even in emptiness, even in darkness, there is always a flicker of light. Do not despair. By holding fast to God in your heart you will be balanced. Any dimension of yourself is a dimension of God's. None of it is yours, anyway.

And like a black hole, I pull the spiritual mindedness from out others who pass by. I help their hearts to quicken, their souls to realign with their own higher selves and purpose.

That same Self as all selves.

That same purpose, to be drawn home.

Why Creation Took a Chance on Mankind

Essentially, what we are doing here in this life, is becoming.

If we are becoming, as individuals and as a civilization, what propels this becoming?

It is creation.

If we are not creating our lives, someone else is doing it, those around us, our government, mass media, bosses, spouses or friends. It's a question of who is in control – who is the manipulator.

But we also control and manipulate ourselves. The more awareness we have that we create our lives, the more manipulative we become, until pretty soon we have squeezed out every last bit of spontaneity. We intellectually calculate our every action. Our hearts become weighty with all the proper and responsible decisions we must make. We can't let go. But if you don't take a chance once in a while, you will dry up. Chance taking is necessary for big ideas to produce big results in the creative process.

This brings us to the question of the nature of the forces in our lives. How unsystematic or spontaneous are *they*? Isn't there just a wee bit of intentional randomness, of grease in the wheel gears in this mechanism called life, loosening it just enough to turn perfectly?

Creation took a chance on mankind, because It had to let go, relinquish control, or dry up.

A mechanic loves grease.

The Truth Shall Set You Free?

What truth? Whose truth? Why does it set me free? What exactly is free?

Is desiring to be a truth seeker, to know and live universal wisdom, a trap of the ego?

If you became that all-encompassing truth, you wouldn't need or want an ego, wouldn't have an ego, in fact, wouldn't even be "you" anymore. You would be one with the Infinite. So do you really want to be free of ignorance, error thinking, cultural bias, desires, even the desire to know the truth? If it meant there was no more YOU? I think not. We need to strive to be free from shackles, to raise human consciousness, and build a better world. But the ultimate Freedom from the world and ourselves is beyond us and our true goals. Pity.

128

The Name Game

Those that chose Jesus called themselves Christians, and those that chose Muhammad called themselves Muslims, and they fought over this naming. Had they said, "We are all lightworkers, united, the wayshowers, the torchbearers, but each finding our own way," they would have saved the world, had they realized a flame is a flame is a flame.

So, in the new world, when some young people said, "We reject all these organized groups" and jokingly said, "We call ourselves Zendorphins, for Zen and endorphins!" I thought, *here we go again*! They're calling themselves *other* again. Saying, "We are not them, but better."

Anytime you say: "I am other and I am better," there is danger. There could even be danger in my saying *this*. To truly be One we must accept that all the variations of light and dark, all the hues of color go together.

So lightworkers and darkworkers play the game, the name-game warfare, to manifest stuff and scenarios in psychological time. Don't we have anything better to do then call names?

Lighten up. Shed it. Drop it. Forget it. No, I don't mean those extra pounds. I mean the resentments, judgments, fears, desires, that luggage that will keep you from making the trip. Go easy on others, go easy on yourself. You will leave it all behind, anyway, so why carry it around?

See no evil/hear no evil/speak no evil monkeys are hanging in our motorhome now. There's more to think about then meets the eye. Does seeing no evil mean closing your eyes to not look, *or* changing your mind to not see anything in the world as evil? To see only the good, or see it as *all* good? And what did the original person who coined the phrase have in mind by "evil?" And who decided what is evil? Shouldn't some evil be seen, exposed, to be rid of it? Like genocide in Africa. Or greenhouse gases.

I like the monkeys. When I think too much, I will recall the term "monkeys on my back", for too many thoughts clamoring for my attention. And I will mentally, gently, carry them over and project them back to the wooden figures. Get them off my back!

February 2008

Where does my will end and God's will begin? Where does God's will end and my will begin? You see the problem with words, and even ideas here.

If I love God, as I perceive the Ultimate to be, with all my heart and soul, and visa versa, are we not each wanting to give of ourselves totally to reinforce the other?

Now, say I'm directed to put aside what I think I *should* do to contribute to the world, and picture the ideal situation for *me*, no obligation to anyone else (including God), how can I do that? When my first desire is to please God and do what I can as His/Her hands and feet and heart on earth?

When we are so intertwined and in love, I don't know where we aren't joined, to separate.

I have no desire to act from self-interest. I have no ego I 'm really stuck to. So if we each feel, "Thy will be my will", it's almost like a silly married couple, trying to please the other more than self, and being at odds about it!

This will be very interesting, and a real dance with the Divine, to see how it comes out!

Must someone win?

I guess at the level of the soul, my highest self knows what it wants and needs. Someone has to make a decision!

I woke up wondering where you have traveled on your spiritual journey this past year. And then I realized. We don't even own the journey! To understand this life is ultimately not mine allows me to quit clinging to all the roles I've adopted, and just go along for the ride.

Remember, the rain is the real blessing; it recycles the oceans, cleans and purifies the air, causes life to grow on the land. The rainbow is merely the ribbon cutting ceremony where we begin anew.

When darkness comes and consumes men's minds and worlds,
Remember, there is always enough light to see by if we gaze within.

When I say "nothing and no one can take my peace from me," I am still in resistance.

Now I say "I create a space for peace to be."

It is not my responsibility, I am not in control. I just am, and peace is.

My Hope

I pray, though I am not a pray-er,
not for things I want, the Universe knows those, if I've read *The Secret*.
How could I ever tell the Universe anything,
as if It didn't know, record, stamp and validate existence.

What I pray for, though I am not a pray-er,
is to remember that each person I meet today
is living a drama, a dream:
half of them are having a bad day, confused/tired/stressed,
half of them are having a fulfilling day,
confused/tired/stressed/challenged/ambitious,
half of them or more don't sleep well,
half of them or more don't love life at its core, at its essence, they only relish
moments,
and half of them or more love life too well, yes that's possible,
for you feel life's misery and suffering, and the earth's pain.
And some of us continually wonder what half we're in.

What I do pray for, in no particular way and to no body of belief,
is that somehow man & womankind can reconnect to loving life again,
arms wide open, expecting nothing, being thankful for everything.

It's time to go along for the ride.
The world will continue to exist without me or you. Honestly.
It's been running Itself for millions of years without you or me,
believe it or not.
Pretend you have control, if your ego enjoys it. Just don't forget you are
playing. And, one minute you're here and the next minute, gone.

So, remember who you meet today, every single person, no one excluded,
the entire functioning of totality from the point of you
is on the ark with you.
And we're past the point of praying, for words don't mean a thing,
and there are no oars.

And the only thing left to do is to share our hearts,
to be kind to others and ourselves.
There can be no regrets,
for time is up.

Only a last chance to fling our arms wide open and love life –
as is –
not offering us any gifts in particular,
just love it for what it is,
and ALL it is,
as the waves take us...

Can we release the needy little me?
To desire only to be desire-less?
Can we let go of the need to control?
And then to let go of the need for letting go?
What is, is.
Let it be.

Tidbits

These were written on other papers, tucked here and there, when my journal wasn't handy. They were jotted down this year, but the exact months are unknown.

Dream ~

A man was hunting me, following me throughout the city and countryside. He would accost me, stab me with a knife, but usually I stabbed him. He was unrelenting; I was always on guard. In time, he diminished in stature, but there continued to be lots of struggles. I had to be violent, or he would stab me. I had no choice. In the end, he was as small as a baby; I put him in a box to hide him, assuming he was dead. I felt the police were looking for me; we were not permitted to rid ourselves of "evil." I was unhappy about the end. It saddened me. I felt spent and empty.

Perhaps we carry "evil" with us at all times, always balancing it, or we "die." To be free from it we are safer, but where is the relief when this "evil" part of us dies? This hints at why we don't let go of duality. We are unnerved by its persistent agitation and life or death situations, but just as uneasy about the void created by its absence.

Maybe a future dream will show me how to live beyond duality, at peace in the void, instead of missing my "evil" twin, my shadow with a knife, that which I have to kill, or allow him to kill me.

I remember I was pursued in another dream, but there was no violence; I stopped, turned, confronted and demanded the evil "Be gone!" It worked.

Do I think I could make peace with, and love this part of me? Of the world? Are we not parts of the same dream? Of the same, the only Oneness? If not for the drama, if life were perfect, maybe we'd become light and go create universes. But we love the drama.

I regret
That I have no regrets.
I decided they were better off dead.
For the whole shebang I give thanks!
I'm using my heart instead of my head.

I am what I am. To seek makes a duality.

Left on a mountaintop, hearts outstretched,
we are the wind beneath each other's wings.

Consciousness is not some "thing",
an object in a field; Consciousness IS the field.

As a Lightworker, let your life be
a testimony for the indwelling Spirit.
Experience Being, which is All That Is.
Connect the dots, the rays of light,
help all become one with the One And Only.
Release your passion for God.

Comfort from Spirit

I was in emotional shock and depression when my aunt died, doing something in the kitchen, and I looked up in an open cupboard to see in big letters: "The One And Only." This is a personal term of endearment I use for God. It made me smile, and feel I was given a hug in the midst of my pain. Later, I looked, and it was the bottom of a Cheerios® Box!

A few days after my aunt died, coming home from a walk, I remembered a neighbor had just moved and suggested I pick any flowers left in her yard. *Maybe some flowers would cheer me up,* I thought, so I detoured by her house. The only kinds of flowers growing were Irises, bushes and bushes of purple Irises, my aunt's favorite flowers! The purple ones are rare, in fact, I'd tried to order some over the Internet to send to my niece, but none were to be found. And here was a whole yard of them, especially for me. I went back 3 different times over the next difficult days and kept them on my table to remind me that I was loved!

Then I got an unsolicited email, and in the subject window it said: "Keep your spirits up, pal." I recognized it was from a card company I knew, so I opened it. It had a little angel, and it said: "I'll be just fine with friends like you." No kidding. It was a message from my aunt through Spirit to cheer me up.

Dreams ~

I feel I am to make some connection with Eastern mysticism from India.

I already mentioned the white rose presented to me by a young boy from India, in a dream on Easter morning, where he gently said: "This is for you; maybe you can gift it to others."

Six months later, I had another dream, of a withered old man from India. He wore white sheeting, and came up to a row of people sitting on the floor who were watching a big television. I was in the middle. He bent down and gave a quick, loose hug to Chris who sat on my left. Then he bent down to hug me, our heads together and cheeks touching, and enormous waves of peace engulfed me. I became aware of nothing but the present moment, no thoughts, just stillness and joy. When he stood up, I remained entranced for an eternal thirty seconds, before "reality" started to flood my consciousness with "normal" perceptions. Again, he bent down and put his head and cheek next to mine, one arm loosely on my shoulder, and gifted me with the same, even deeper sensation of tranquility and happiness.

I understood that *this* state of consciousness was Ultimate Reality, and original normality.

The old man sat down on my right side. Soon, like a squirming child, he wiggled his upper torso into my lap, laying his head on my legs, like a big dog who tries to be a lap dog but only fits halfway. Then, to get my attention from the world, he reached up his skinny arm and covered my eyes with his hand so I couldn't watch the television. He was lovable and child-

144

like, but still the withered old man. I understood his playful gesture to be blocking my absorption of belief in the worldview propagated by the media. He didn't want it to taint my perception. It was a clear message to stop watching television – and I did.

This is curious to me, since I have no link with India. Although, I like the Goddess Shiva (with all the arms) who represents destruction and creation both; and the non-dualistic nature of Reality, seeing both sides to everything and accepting everything. I also appreciate the Hindu myth about Supreme Consciousness exploding into creation and losing Itself, only to let the pieces be drawn together again. I guess I'll check out the India connection. How hard can *"There is nothing but consciousness"* be to figure out?

I see the Hindu myth of a hide-and-seek God playing out in our individual lives, as well as the Creator's. Our story-dramas are the vehicles through which our growing souls travel. We build ourselves up over a lifetime, collecting all the puzzle pieces, finding our own way, and locating all parts of self, only to release it all in the end.

We were one with ALL THAT IS, up to the end.

But then, the "with" part dissolves, and we become the ONE, the ALL THAT IS.

No separation exists in the end.

Keepers of the Flame

My days are wedged between luminous heart-kindling sunrises and sunsets, and as I watch for unspeakable colors, one thing is certain:

By grace of the Eternal Presence, "I Am" is here, as me.
I become the "I Am" made manifest.
My debt is to choose joy. I'll be a candle in the flame of life,
ready to re-ignite all other light in a passion celebration,
a dance of Life lovers.
If all people reverently greeted the sunrise or sunset,
happiness would emanate from a planet of love. It's just that simple.

What is life?
Life is a puzzle, solve it.
Life is a mystery, unwrap it.
Life is a maze, go through it.
Life is a story, tell it.
Life is a sport, win it.
Life is a song, sing it.
Life is a flower, smell it.
Life is touch, feel it.
Life is an offer, take it.
Life is love, love it.

God never forgives you because God never judges you.
He gave us freewill, so he wouldn't punish us for using it creatively.

If you forgive everyone for everything as situations arise,
you save nothing inside you that has to be forgiven down the road.
This adds to living in grace.

You have a right to hold onto resentments,
but it's like keeping something rotten inside you.

If you have a choice between being right or being kind, choose kind.

Before you get up in the morning, say, " I am available to more good than I
have ever experienced, realized or imagined before.
I am thankful for _____ I apologize for _____."
See how your life is transformed.

That's All, Folks

The universe is an intelligent, mysterious and loving ground of Being. Another name is: All That Is. There is an *Is*-ness to me, as well. I am Being, being *me*. God at the point of me!

In a silly movie, *You, Me and Dupree*, a goofy guy named Dupree was concerned about his roommate, Greg, who wasn't acting like his usual self. What had happened to his friend's core personality? He called it his *Greg*-ness. Greg's life was going wrong because he wasn't being his authentic self. The existential point was made. We each have a higher self blueprint. I have a *Cindy*-ness.

In the end of the movie, as only Hollywood can do, Dupree, a former unemployed drifter, became a popular motivational speaker, a self-help guru for personal development helping thousands of people!

Living *Is* the Dream World

I wander this life of dream,
sometimes on the edge of awakening,
but no hurry.
The landscapes of nature are enchanting.
The situations with fellow travelers are challenging.
When fear, stress or pain enter the scene
I remind myself "It is only a dream!" and continue on through adventures.
Sometimes I want to wake, it might be more peaceful.

When I do slightly rouse myself, I feel a tingling warmth,
but strange immobility.
There is nothing to do when you are fully alive,
nothing to want, to need, to achieve, to become.

If the secret answer to life is that it exists, period,
as a roaming shadow between the oneness of dream and not-dream,
culminating in realization of consciousness,
then I guess I'll choose to dream a while longer.

I'll follow my ultimate path: to climb the highest mountain peak,
unafraid of disappearing,
knowing I will become God again,
then enter another dream, just to sleep for a while.

154

Bless Yourself By Giving

"One of the most difficult things to give away is kindness; it usually comes back to you." ~ Anonymous

Sure you've heard giving is a virtuous activity. But did you know it's one of the best things to do for *yourself*? Giving is as rewarding to the giver as to those who receive. And I don't mean just giving money.

When two weeks of Christmas company left, I relaxed alone beneath the stars in my swirling spa. I reverberated from days of cooking, cleaning, sightseeing and parties. I felt completely drained, rummy with fatigue, yet brimming with exultation. *What is this paradox,* I thought, *feeling empty yet full at the same time?*

I began thinking about giving and receiving. I watched the procession of water in the spa, swiftly flowing into the filters, then out the jets, circulating over and over. This is how the law of giving and receiving operates, I reflected. It's all one process that must keep going to enrich our lives. Yet sometimes, we don't want to give, thinking it takes away time or energy from ourselves. We operate like clogged spa filters, creating a stagnant movement of energy in our lives.

I had exhausted myself by giving to my family and friends. I now see that the more I gave, the more I received. I found joy in their happiness: I watched them lounge in pajamas until noon, play board games, wrestle, laugh and giggle. I was blanketed with warm hugs. Their smiles, brimming with affection and appreciation, emblazoned my heart. One highlight was a thank you note left behind on my pillow, "Thank you for sharing your home, Christmas, cheer and love!" After reading it, my heart jumped all day.

Psychologists agree, we can increase our happiness and become less self-centered by simply giving of ourselves: a helping hand, an ear for listening, or even a smile. Mother Theresa, the infinite-hearted giver, reassured us: *"It is not how much we give but how much love we put into giving."*

A Master Psychologist said, *"...love thy neighbor..."* When we hold compassion in our hearts and do kind deeds, we are filling ourselves as well as others with joy! The greatest gift we can give ourselves is giving to others. And if we give so earnestly that we become empty from our giving, we have made room for pure undiluted life to pour into our spirits. *"They give as in yonder valley the myrtle breathes its fragrance into space. Through the hands of such as these God speaks, and from behind their eyes He smiles upon the earth. For in truth, it is life that gives unto life, while you who deem yourself a giver are but a witness."* ~ Kahlil Gibran

Now I understand the paradox of feeling empty yet full. It was a moment of mindfulness, of realizing the simultaneous flow of giving and receiving. I had unknowingly blessed myself, and found that those who give of themselves receive the fullest of life's blessings. Remember, your good is unfolding with your every unselfish or random act of kindness. It's okay that you know giving is one of the best things to do for yourself!

From a tea bag: THE MOMENT YOU LOVE, YOU ARE UNLIMITED.

"God's will" = a freewill universe.

God's Reality = all realities, everything we acknowledge
and can yet imagine.

Since we are a part of God and visa versa (there is only perceived separation), we are enmeshed in the infinite matrix of Reality. This is a beautiful picture: God is everywhere in all there is, in our being and spirit, and we reside in that totality. We are as significant as any other cause or effect in the functioning of the Universe! If your heart is open, this should give you goosebumps.

I realized at Unity today, that I do not have love - I Am Love.
A builder of bridges, leaping between islands of consciousness,
bringing us all into one consciousness.

Love is contagious, catchy, like an electrical current charging from one to
another... It could circle the earth.

The I Am that is Love, that is I, and thee, is also guilty of wanting.
But It wants only this: for all to exist in love.

So catch the wave, ride the shooting star.
Arrive in any manner as soon as possible,
to fulfill our common destiny and purpose - to be Love.

No words
no words
no words.

Get to that place where no words are on your tongue or in your mind
and you are home.

I dreamed that I woke up from a dream.
And then, I woke up from *that* dream.
Or did I?

That Place

I wish for you to find that place within yourself,
where you don't need anyone or anything.
That center of stillness,
which the world can't invade.
And to go there as often as you can.
That is your refuge.
That is your answer to pain.
It is a space that is not yours personally,
but a place all Masters have been,
and is there for you to share,
and lay down in repose.

The world will never give you what you want.
It only fuels the wanting of your ego
for more, other, better, me and mine.
This tiny self is never happy.
Your only happiness will come when you know you are a part of the bigger
Self.
The only peace you will have, and it's not to be earned someday
but is yours *today* if you really want it,
is to enter that place within,
in awe,
with respect,

with love in your heart
and a clear quiet mind.
Humbly ask to rest there,
listen with all your attention
and you will feel loved.

There is no greater feeling than this,
no other calling more urgent.
The world may be a game on many levels,
but that sacred silent place is where reality and divinity exist side by side
in their purest essence,
and *your* purest Essence.

Becoming Conscious Through Love

He recognized himself in his son, as they both grew older.

When his son was born, and the two of them spent hours rocking together, soothing one another's hearts, he felt this connection. But he also recognized something else... the Divine in his son.

He recognized himself and the Divine also in other people. More and more, in everyone he met.

As himself, he saw in them his actions, his mistakes, his affections, his ways, his positive thinking and his error thinking. His quaintness, his passions, his fears.

He saw in them the Divine, those times they used their hands, hearts and minds to help one another, to nurture and support each other. They were holy in that contentedness; they glowed with gratitude, and loved life.

Then, in his not too old age, he began to see his own humanness and his own divinity, and to see that they were finally merging into the One being he was meant to be living. Joined at the hip with humanity, joined at the heart with God, he saw the whole picture, and felt the glory of this scenario for all mankind.

It all began when he saw and felt himself in his son, in that rocking chair, and watched the universe speak from his eyes aglow, he who had just come from there. And his father's heart had cracked open, to release the imprisoned splendor.

The love of a parent is the most true and unconditional in those early years, when life is pure and the Oneness is felt in that love. The same

Oneness, the same Love, that pours on us, that gifts and blesses us, that we don't own, is not ours, but comes through us, of which all life is a part.

Through love, the father had become a conscious part.

The Question on Everyone's Mind: What Next?

Many of us have chosen to board the ark of rising consciousness.

Once the small light goes on within our hearts, we are drawn into consciousness, like the moth to the flame. We are the moth *and* the flame!

We join the One And Only, the All That Is, in a variety of playful ways.

We are aligned with the world that is rising, and not the world that is falling, though we often stand with one foot in each world.

My question is:

Will we wake up one day with accelerated awareness, but a stranger in our own skin?

And will our familiar picture of reality be shattered into a million puzzle pieces, with no possibility of recognition or re-assembly?

Is the new earth: those ascending to a 4th or 5th dimension, co-habiting the earth with those still struggling in the third dimension?

At some point, do we surrender, and give up *everything* in order to evolve, and just… step into the other side?

Then there's the related question. Is our planet herself ascending?

Do you feel the 2012 scenario is pointing to the cosmic future?

A myth I heard, kind of like Sleeping Beauty, is that the Source of Being and non-being, the unimaginable Oneness, is sleeping, until awakened to a heavenly existence *someday*. It is lost in Its role, Its outer purpose, in the dream of life, of us, in a dance of opposites. Perhaps It selected the button "surprise me!" and It became the worlds.

So, kissed by the Spirit, we are all awakening, the universe, the earth, people, the Divinity within All! Together again. At last. A totality of inner purpose exploding into joy and peace. That *someday*... is now!

So here's the main question.

What next?

Where does this culmination of consciousness lead? For mankind? For the earth?

A final point. If I fear I am not good enough to go, that is my ego.
If I really don't care if I go or not, perhaps I am free enough to go.

Moses Moments

Someone who read my book said, "You are very close to God right now."

I took it as the highest compliment, since it's where I hope I Am.

"Be careful," they warned.

Is this why spiritual seekers are *seeking* God, as their chosen role?

Because to remove the veil, to actually find God, as Moses did on the mountain, could be dangerous?

Now that's funny! To be afraid of God!

If getting too close to the burning bush is what Moses, or God in Moses wanted, it would have happened, and he would have burned up, and spirit gone to...Duuuh! To where he had sought. Journey over. Game points won. Mission accomplished.

So. We are to remain the firefly. Icarus circling the sun with a purpose.

If we are content in that, we honor God by being the servant, the testimony, as the light always represents the fire.

Presence is Being on the mountaintop within.

And no warning will hold my heart back from soaring.

When you find that deep stillness,
words forming thoughts on the screen are a vague but messy ripple,
annoying,
even slightly painful.
Like my breath, I rise and fall, rise and fall, always resting a while in the
stillness throughout the day, the place with no words.
When you find that place at Center,
a negative thought actually hurts,
a doubt seems disrespectful,
a resentment seems to turn around and jump back on you,
a less than perfect vision seems so wrong, and potentially destructive.

What is uttered in our hearts in that silence is sacred creation.
We see our responsibility.
And all that surfaces that we call "less than perfect,"
all that sends ripples out on the water is needed for existence.
For duality reality is born and revolves around the stillness
in waves of Life manifesting.
We create our own waves called the life we know.
But all of us know that stillness, as well.
And it is all holy. It is all God.

The Dream Called Living

To understand non-duality, wondering where the dream ends and reality begins, I see that they are joined, inseparable, One, All Life.

Dreams become more real, and reality more dream-like, and anything is possible.

Life goes on endlessly,
with or without form.
And with or without my awareness in this very instant.
Am I running to catch the train?
Or am I already on it, and just don't know it?

By God's Grace I have awakened,
and by God's Grace I will be put where I need to go.

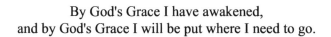

We're on a magical mystery tour. The Beatles got it right!

There is no *reason* for life. Life has a propensity, a yearning to exist.
The answer to life is life itself.

You Have the Key

You have the key to your own life.
The answers are all there that you need,
the words in the ways you need to hear them.
And being the key, you can unlock and see,
that life is not a mystery,
but the simple stuffing and essence of eternity.

Experience

Being

About the Author

Cindy writes to touch your deepest self, who is not you at all, and unite the pieces of the One. "I feel consciousness is accelerating now, and Lightworkers and frequency-holders, such as those who read this book, are coalescing in order to ride the waves together. It is a wonderful time to be alive! Our steadfast creative thoughts for a new earth will produce miracles, if we do not waver in our vision."

Retired to the White Mountains of Arizona near the Apache Reservation, Cindy walks the rim trail most days, and explores dirt roads with her faithful old truck. Previously, she lived on a small houseboat for 5 years, where one of her sons was born. Then she raised three sons, while living on a creek for 15 years. All three sons are in the Coast Guard. She has a background as communications coordinator, editor-in-chief of a mass-marketed quarterly newsletter, librarian, teacher, and photojournalist.